DIFFERENCES BETWEEN JOHN AND THE SYNOPTIC GOSPELS

By

DR. JACK R. NEUBAUER

ACKNOWLEDGMENTS

As I look back over a project like this, I realize that many people played crucial parts in the writing and deserve to be thanked publicly.

First, I'd like to express my appreciation to Dr. James Kallas and all the Professors at the California Graduate School of Theology in Glendale, California, for inspiring me to go deeper in my studies.

Of course I also wish to express my appreciation to my wife, Darlene, who was invaluable as usual, coordinating the project from beginning to end. She kept me going, kept me organized, and translated my handwriting. Also our grateful appreciation to our dear friend Rev. Bob Whaley, Pastor of First Baptist Church in Joshua Tree, California, who did the final proofing.

My thanks also to friends at Hope Baptist Church in Phoenix, Arizona, for their encouragement in getting started.

For all of those who have played a part in creating this book, I pray you will be encouraged and built up in your walk with the Lord and in your ministries. God bless you!

Jack Neubauer

It is with great pleasure that I recommend this writing to you. The author, Jack Neubauer, is an outstanding student of God's word, so his thoughts on the Gospels will reflect on the authors keen insights.

I have spent many hours discussing scripture as we fellowshipped over lunch. Your time in reading this book will prove valuable to the knowledge of the Gospels.

Rev. Wes Baker

Dr. Jack Neubauer came to the Morongo Valley to write a book in his retirement. However, he was soon called into service as pastor of Community Baptist Church of Morongo Valley (now Church of the Lighted Cross). The book was soon put on a back burner.

This is how I became acquainted with Pastor Jack. I served as pastor of Joshua Tree First Baptist Church. Both churches were part of the Desert Baptist Association, so we often sat together at meetings and attended the same association and regional gatherings. We even celebrated annual DBA pastors Christmas dinners and fellowship in our homes.

Pastor Jack and I enjoyed discussing pastor stuff and theology. He would describe his recent book with excitement. I couldn't quite put it all together. Then the Neubauer's moved to Phoenix and pastored there for several years. How happy I was when they announced that they were moving back to Morongo Valley. The Morongo Valley church had fallen on hard times, so Jack felt led to do what he could to revive this church. Using humor, a puppet named Zeke, and good old fashioned preaching while experiencing diminished physical energies, he once again energized the church, naming it Church of the Lighted Cross.

Somehow during all these years Jack completed his book. It was my pleasure to receive a rough draft copy, which I was asked to edit. Sixteen months after Jack's death it was my delight to hear from Darlene Neubauer, who asked me to write this forward for "Differences Between the Synoptic Gospels and John". She had been encouraged to publish the book.

The Synoptic Gospels can be set alongside each other for easy comparison. John's Gospel cannot be so easily compared. There is no hint in the Fourth Gospel that John was attempting to either complement or correct the other three. How can the differences be explained? This is the issue Dr. Jack Neubauer addresses in his book.

May the Lord bless Jack's efforts and those who read it to further their understanding.

Rev. Bob Whaley

First Published by

GrievingTeensPublishing.com
PO Box 14370
Palm Desert, CA 92255

ISBN 978-1-105-28761-9

TABLE OF CONTENTS

CHAPTER 1

Importance of the Book

Anyone who has done a serious study of the Gospel of John and then sought to compare that Gospel with Matthew, Mark and Luke, found that they were immediately confronted with many differences.

Over the years, I have studied all the Gospels and this has increased my interest in how others were handling these differences, both in their teaching and in their sermons. To my surprise, most of the people consulted have never made an honest effort to have some answer for these differences. Furthermore, I have not been able to locate any books that speak to the one problem of these differences.

The importance of this book is to look at these differences and to give some kind of answer as to why they are there rather than continue to ignore the problem.

Questions to be Answered

In examining the differences between the Synoptics and John, I will seek to answer the question, "What was the Fourth Gospel saying to the church of the Evangelist's day?" "The differences between John and the Synoptics must not be glossed over."[1] It is generally assumed that the Gospel of John is the simple Gospel.

[1] 1 George Eldon Ladd, A Theology of the New Testament, (Michigan: Eerdmans, 1979), p.215.

But as this book is read, it will become very clear that this is the most profound Gospel out of the four, and could very well be the most profound book of the entire New Testament.

Background of the Study

Over the centuries, efforts have been made to show the Life of Christ in some kind of sequence by using all four Gospels. This effort has for the most part been called, the Harmony of the Gospels. This study will discuss special topics, such as: the time of Jesus' birth, the genealogy, Christ at the different Passovers, the Sermon on the Mount, the date of the Last Supper, and chronological questions concerning the resurrection narratives.

Our concern will not be a study in harmonizing the Gospels, but a look at the major events that differ between the Synoptics and John. We will also seek to see how far the Fourth Gospel was dependent on the Synoptics.

Purpose of the Study

The purpose of this study is to do four things: (1) to locate and describe the major differences between the Synoptics and the Gospel of John; (2) to evaluate their differences
and see if they can be reconciled with good research; (3) to see why the Evangelist made these
changes, why he left some events out of his Gospel and why he added new events not recorded in the Synoptics; and finally, (4) this study intends to offer a solution to the problem of why John

deliberately recast and interpreted the life and words of Jesus our Lord.

Statement of the Problem

There are many differences between the Synoptic Gospels and the Gospel of John. These differences are seen in many different ways. They can be seen in the location of the ministry of Christ, the duration of His ministry, His miracles, even down to His very words. The problem one needs to consider is what these differences mean to the New Testament student.

Areas of Contribution

This study will contribute in the following areas:

1. To get a new perspective of the Fourth Gospel in light of the Synoptic Gospels.
2. To look at how scholars over the years have tried to overcome the differences between John and the Synoptics.
3. To share one way that we can understand the differences in the Synoptics for our teaching and preaching today.

Definition of Terms Used in the Study

Synoptic Gospels: Term for the Gospels of Matthew, Mark, and Luke, which are similar in many respects.

Synoptic Problem: Question of the origin, chronology, and various differences, similarities, and relationships of the three Gospels of Matthew, Mark, and Luke.

The Evangelist: This is a reference to the author of the Gospel of John.

Dualism: The dualism in the Synoptic Gospels is primarily horizontal; a contrast between two ages—this age and the Age to come. The dualism of John is primarily vertical; a contrast between two worlds—the world above and the world below.

Satan-ward View: This view is a description of the work of Christ in light of how it deals with Satan.

God-ward View: This view is a description of the work of Christ in light of what God wanted accomplished for Himself.

Eschatology: Study of the last things. Eschatology in this book involves the final coming and triumph of Christ and His Kingdom, and sometimes the resurrection and related topics.

Diatessaron: "Through four" (Greek meaning). The harmony of the four Gospels prepared by Tation in the second century. He wove the narratives of Matthew, Mark, and Luke along with John into a single account of the life of Christ.

Delimitation's and Limitations of the Study

This study is subject to the following delimitation's:

1. We will not take into account the proof of the authorship of the Gospel of John. We will assume that John, son of Zebedee, brother of James, was the author. In the main body of this work, however, the reader will be convinced that John the Apostle was indeed the author of this Gospel in some form.

2. We will not go chapter by chapter to look at the differences between John and the Synoptics. This study will not take the form of a commentary.

3. This book will be limited to the material dealing only with the fundamental and far-reaching differences between the Gospel of John and the Synoptic Gospels. In some cases, a warning must be given to the reader that will over-state the case, but it will be done for a purpose. The purpose will be seen as the conclusions are drawn.

Organization of the Study

For an overview of the study, look carefully at the earlier portion of Chapter One. There the reader will find the statement of the problem being considered, the background of the study, and the importance of the study.

Chapter Two presents twelve fundamental and far ranging differences in the Gospel of John and the Synoptics. These differences will be stated clearly so that at once the reader is being confronted with the reason for the overall subject.

Chapter Three describes some of the current efforts as to how to harmonize these differences.

Chapter Four contains a description in detail of how John sometimes corrects away from history and at other times he is correcting toward history.

Chapter Five summarizes the findings and draws conclusions showing how I interpret what the Apostle John was trying to do with his material. There will be some examples of interpretation of entire chapters and of some of the signs of Jesus and how John changed them and why.

CHAPTER 2

Twelve Differences between John and the Synoptics

As the reader looks at the fundamental differences between the Gospel of John and the Synoptic Gospels, he will begin to see the real value of this book and come to understand its worth and purpose.

The place to begin is with the question, "What is one of the first Bible verses people learn to memorize?" Of course, it is John 3:16. This is one of the first verses given to Sunday school children, and the very fact that this verse is put in their hands first of all, before giving them any other scripture, would seem to suggest that the Gospel of John is simple, placid and a calm pool upon which the great truths of God float. But I would suggest to the reader, nothing is further from the truth. The more one delves into the Gospel of John the more one begins to recognize it is not a calm, untroubled pool, but rather a turbulent, problematic, troublesome book. And everywhere one looks, he finds differences of interpretation.

Therefore, this chapter will be confined to the problems. The place to begin is by emphasizing the point that at every conceivable step of Jesus' ministry there is a difference between John and the first three Gospels. It is time now to begin to look at these differences one by one. The reader must keep an open mind and be in prayer as he goes forward. First of all there are:

The Differences between John and the Synoptics In the Location of Jesus' Ministry

Looking at the ministry of Jesus as it unfolds in the Synoptics, it can be seen that Jesus was primarily a man of the north. (Mark. 1:9) One sees this in reading where He did some of His preaching and where He accomplished some of His miracles. This is called His "Galilean Ministry." These events took place in the cities of Capernaum, Cana, Nazareth, etc.

As a matter of fact, the Gospels of Matthew, Mark, and Luke show the ministry of Jesus as so exclusively confined to the north that when He came to the south for the first time, His message and His mighty works had preceded Him, and it would seem the people in the south had never seen Him before. But they had heard about how He was able to still the storm, cast out the demons, raise the dead and heal the sick. Therefore, when He finally came down to the south they went wild in a burst of joy, a delirium of delight to see him and they actually gave Him a tickertape parade. That day is called Palm Sunday.

They said, "Here He is! Here is the man we heard about." They rolled out the red carpet. They said, "We heard about Him, now He is here. We can see Him in action. If He could do all those wonderful and powerful miracles in the north, maybe He can do even more here in the south. Perhaps He can overthrow our enemies and get the boot of Rome off our neck." They addressed Him as Son of David, because David was the greatest warrior of all their heroes. Here was the man perhaps that could repeat

David's great victories. That is the way the Synoptics unroll. Jesus was basically a man of the north.

However, when one looks at the Gospel of John there is a completely different picture. Look at John 4:43-45: "Now after two days he departed thence, and went into Galilee." He made a quick trip up to Galilee, which is in the north. Where had He been? He had been in the south. Just read the context. Now look at John 4:44: "For Jesus himself testified, that a prophet hath no honor in his own country." Where is a prophet poorly received? In his own land. Look at verse 45: "Then when He was come into Galilee, the Galileans received Him." Now if He got a warm welcome in Galilee, and that is in the north, when He had already said that a prophet is not well received in his own country, that implies that Galilee was not His own country. When you read on you see that the bulk of Jesus' ministry in the Gospel of John was performed in the south. There were a couple of miracles up in the north, but the major part of Jesus' ministry unfolded in the south.

So that is one fundamental difference. Matthew, Mark and Luke show Jesus as a man of the north and the Gospel of John show Jesus as a man of the south. Jesus Himself claimed to be a man of the south. I will come back to this first difference when I show how this can be harmonized.

The Differences Between John and the Synoptics Regarding the Length of Jesus' Ministry

Another difference concerns the length of Jesus' ministry. How long did the ministry of Jesus last? Most will be quick to reply, "About three years." The reason they can say this is that they have been reading the Gospel of John.

Albert Schweitzer, in his famous book, The Quest of the Historical Jesus, presents an argument, which has never really received full and adequate recognition. Albert Schweitzer's argument is this: If one only had the Gospel of Mark, (Period! Only Mark)... If he were not reading Mark looking over his shoulder at John all the time… If he had never seen John and only had Mark and someone were to ask him that same question, "How long did the ministry of Jesus last?"… Does the reader know what the answer would be? The ministry of Jesus lasted less than a year.[1] There was a kind of frantic intensity to the Gospel of Mark. Time seems to be of the absolute essence. What are the two words that describe Jesus' ministry in the Gospel of Mark? They are "immediately" and "straightway." The Greek word is euthus—and then—and then, and then.

If one takes a pen and opens to chapter one of Mark and underlines the two words "immediately" and "straightway," he will see them in the King James Version some eight times alone. As William L. Lane says in the commentary on the Gospel of Mark: The word "straightway" is a Marcan term which occurs between forty and fifty times in the Gospel. It is appropriate to translate "at once."[2]

1 Albert Schweitzer, The Quest of the Historical Jesus, (New York: MacMillan, 1948).
2 William L. Lane, Commentary on the Gospel of Mark, (Michigan: Eerdmans, 1974).

There seems to be a frantic, breathless pace to the Gospel of Mark. The reader gets the feeling that Jesus was living with the conviction that the end of the world was upon them. So the Gospel of Mark seems to be an abbreviated ministry. This is seen also in the fact that it is short. It is not only short, but it seems to be breathless. It is like they were living in the very last days!

Now, compare this to what one finds in the Gospel of John. On three different occasions (John 2:13; 5:1; and 7:10) the fourth Gospel speaks of the Feast of the Jews being at hand. In Jewish thought, if one is talking about the Feast of the Jews, without any further qualification, he is talking about The Feast! The most important one would be the Feast of the Passover. So, from these texts one knows that John is talking about the annual Feast of the Passover three times. The context makes it clear that he is talking about three different Feasts of the Passover.

If Jesus lived through three Feasts of the Passover, how many years did His ministry last? The answer is at least two and perhaps as many as four. Using the Gospel of John, and using the three references to the different Passovers, scholars have concluded that the ministry lasted over several years, not just a brief span of a few months. Therefore, if the Synoptics can be called breathless and eschatological, looking for the end of the age, then John would have to be called a non-eschatology, or to use a term used by scholars today, a "Realized Eschatology." The Gospel of John does not look for the end in the immediate future. That is the whole point of a little conversation which unfolds in the last chapter of John between Jesus and Peter. Jesus told Peter he was going to die (John 21:18,19). So Peter said, "OK, I'm going to die, but what about John over there, is he going to die?" Then notice what Jesus said:

> Jesus saith unto him, "If I will that he tarry till I come, what is that to thee? Follow thou me." Then went this saying abroad among the brethren, that that disciple should not die: yet Jesus said not unto him, he shall not die; but, if I will that he tarry till I come, what is that to thee? (John 21:21-22)

There was an early tradition that Jesus would return before the death of the apostle John. Therefore, taking Mark 9:1 literally, when was the end of the world supposed to come? Answer: In the lifetime of the disciples. When the disciple got older, the people began to wonder if this was going to be an unanswered or unfulfilled prophecy. John is speaking precisely to that point. "The saying went abroad among the brethren, that that disciple should not die: Yet Jesus said not unto him, he should not die." Jesus did not say he was not to die. John tell us, do not necessarily look for the end of the world in the lifetime of the apostles. John is speaking to that problem. The Gospel of John is what one calls "Realized Eschatology,"

The Differences Between John and The Synoptics on Just Who Jesus Is

Another difference between the Synoptics and John's Gospel is when the disciples learn who Jesus really is. Looking at the Synoptics, let the reader go to a place called Caesarea Philippi, which is in the north, about one hundred miles from Jerusalem. What took place there according to Matthew 16? Jesus began to ask the disciples a series of questions. "Gentlemen, what is the word going around about me, who are the people saying I am?" Then came the response from Peter, spokesman for the group. "Everybody is pretty impressed with you Jesus." That is a free translation, but that is about what is intended. "Everybody thinks you are a prophet, some have even said that you are Elijah, some have concluded that you are John the Baptist and some say Jeremiah. They are all convinced you are a great man of God." So Jesus moved on to question two. "I don't want to know only what the people are saying, I want to know what you think. Who do you say that I am?" Peter again answered for the group saying, "The Christ, son of the living God." Matthew 16:17 says: "And Jesus answered and said unto him, blessed art thou, Simon Bar-jona; for flesh and blood hath not revealed it unto thee, but my Father which is in heaven."

"Good work Peter, your eyes have been opened, at last you finally realize who I am." Peter began to see the full dimension of who this person Jesus really is. He was not just an ordinary prophet, but He is the Son of God. At Caesarea Philippi then, one of the critical things that happened is that the disciples, led by the Spirit, learned fully who Jesus is.

The Synoptics say that from the beginning they did not know fully who Jesus is. This shows up clearly in Mark 4:41. "And they feared exceedingly, and said one to another, What manner of man is this, that even the wind and the sea obey him?" Jesus stilled the storm and what did the disciples say? "What manner of man is this?" In other words, "My goodness, who is this guy, even nature obeys Him." They left all to follow Him, but they still were not clear about just who He really is.

It is clear then, that at Caesarea Philippi they learned who He really is. The disciples then knew through the Spirit that Jesus is the Son of God. When they discovered who Jesus is, then Jesus could go on and tell them what He must do. Look at Matthew 16:21:

> From that time forth began Jesus to show unto his disciples, how that he must go unto Jerusalem, and suffer many things of the elders and chief priests and scribes, and be killed, and be raised again the third day.

May I remind the reader of something that many often overlook. Notice the first three words of that verse. From that time! What time is being talked about? It is Caesarea Philippi. From Caesarea Philippi onward, when they learned who Jesus really is, from that time Jesus told His disciples that He must go up to Jerusalem and suffer and die. But, on the third day He would rise. So it is only as of Caesarea Philippi that Jesus could begin to teach His disciples that He must suffer and die in order to win the victory over Satan. And if one reads carefully the story of Christ's trip down to Jerusalem, he finds that the disciples still were not all that clear on what Jesus meant about the Kingdom. (Mark. 10:35-45) So, at Caesarea Philippi two very important events take place:

1. The disciples learned fully who Jesus is.
2. From that time forward Jesus could tell them that he must die.

Prior to this time in the Synoptics Jesus had not clearly told His disciples that he must die. This is made clear by the reaction of Peter when he heard the prediction of Jesus' death for the first time. See what happened in Matthew 16:22-23:

> Then Peter took him, and began to rebuke him, saying, "Be it far from thee Lord, this shall not be unto thee." But he turned, and said unto Peter, "Get thee behind me, Satan, thou art an offense unto me, for thou savorest not the things that be of God, but those that be of men."

Peter said, "Wait a minute Lord, don't you talk about dying! You can't die." This was the first time Peter learned this news. But what did Christ have to say to Peter? "Get thee behind me Satan."

The point is that Caesarea Philippi, in the Synoptics, is absolutely critical in the ministry of Jesus. Only afterward did he tell of His impending death and the disciples learned for the first time that Jesus is the Christ.

To come to the counterpoint, Caesarea Philippi is not even mentioned in John. It simply is not there. Instead, there is a whole different outlook on the life of Christ. When in the Synoptics did the disciples learn who Jesus is? At Casearea Philippi. But what had already taken place in John, chapter one? Take a look at what Andrew said when he went to find his brother Peter:

> One of the two, which heard John, speak, and followed him, was Andrew, Simon Peter's brother. He first findeth his own brother

> Simon, and saith unto him, "We have found the Messiah", which is, being interpreted, the Christ. (John 1:40-41)

So, what has happened? Already in chapter one in the Gospel of John the disciples knew that this Jesus is the Messiah, the Christ. As a matter of fact, it was not Peter who announced it, but it was Peter who was told that fact by his brother Andrew.

These are differences that must be faced. Some kind of answer must be given to these differences and they shall be given in a later chapter. What I am doing here is laying the problems before the reader.

To carry this a step further, in the Synoptics the disciples learned who Jesus is at Caesarea Philippi. But in John chapter one, not only did the disciples know that Jesus is the Christ, but in chapter four even the outsiders know who Jesus is. There does not seem to be a mystery. We see this as we look at the story of the Samaritan woman:

> They said unto the woman, now we believe, not because of thy saying, for we have heard him ourselves, and know that this is indeed the Christ, the Savior of the world. (John 4:42)

Does the reader see what this verse is saying? Even the hated Samaritans, the outsiders, know who Jesus is. In John's Gospel there is a whole different point of view beginning to emerge here. Why? We will look at this later.

In going just a step further, one of the basic differences between John's Gospel and the Synoptics is that in John's Gospel

Jesus is omniscient. He knows all things. (John 6:64) He has divine knowledge of everyone and everything. That is not clear and it is not stated in the Synoptics. There is then a different point of view regarding the life of Jesus in John from that which is found in Matthew, Mark and Luke.

The Differences Between John and the Synoptics As to What Set Off the Jews to Move Against Jesus, to Take His Life

Another difference between John and the Synoptics must be considered. The turning point in the life of Jesus was Caesarea Philippi in the Synoptics. As I brought out before, the focus of Jesus' direction after Caesarea Phillipi was toward His death in Jerusalem. Therefore, He set His face to go toward Jerusalem. But upon arriving at Jerusalem, the people gave Jesus the welcome that is today celebrated as Palm Sunday, as was mentioned above. Because of Jesus' popularity, the Jews hesitated to move against Him at this point for fear of the crowds. So what did Jesus do at this point? Did He just rest in His popularity and allow His ministry to continue to prosper? No! Instead, it seems that He headed almost directly to cleanse the Temple to further irritate the Jews. Perhaps Jesus was deliberately attempting to force their hand.

In Matthew 21, this can be seen quite clearly. In verses one to eleven, the story of the triumphal entry is related, and then immediately after it in verse twelve we find:

> "And Jesus went into the Temple of God, and cast out all them that sold and bought in the temple, and overthrew the tables of the moneychangers, and the seats of them that sold doves."

Following this we find the reaction of the leaders of the people.

> "And when the chief priests and scribes saw the wonderful things that he did, and the children crying in the temple, and saying, Hosanna to the son of David; they were <u>sore displeased.</u>" (Matthew 21:15)

In the Synoptics, the story of the cleansing of the temple takes on tremendous significance. Perhaps if Jesus had not taken this aggressive action here, His ministry would have been greatly extended, but instead it appears to be the final turning point from a popular prophet to one who can be crucified. In the Gospel of John, however, this event of the cleansing of the temple is moved to the very early part of the story. Can the reader determine from a careful study of the Gospel of John what the turning point was in this Gospel? The springboard that led to Christ's death in John obviously was not the cleansing of the Temple. It was rather the raising of Lazarus in the eleventh chapter that precipitated the hostilities of the Jews and lead to the cross. Look at John eleven. Skip over the Lazarus story and begin with verse 45 through verse 54.

> Then many of the Jews, which came to Mary, and had seen the things which Jesus did, believed on him. But some of them went their ways to the Pharisees, and told them what things Jesus had done. Then gathered the chief priests and

the Pharisees a council, and said, "What do we?" for this man doeth many miracles. If we let him thus alone, all men will believe on him: and the Romans shall come and take away both our place and nation. And one of them, named Caiaphas, being the high priest that same year, said unto them, "Ye know nothing at all, nor consider that it is expedient for us, that one man should die for the people, and that the whole nation perish not." And this spake he not of himself, but being high priest that year, he prophesied that Jesus should die for that nation. And not for that nation only, but that also he should gather together in one the children of God that were scattered abroad. Then from that day forth they took counsel together for to put him to death. Jesus therefore walked no more openly among the Jews, but went thence unto a country near to the wilderness, into a city called Ephraim, and there continues with his disciples. So began a plot to kill Jesus. "If Jesus keeps up with these great miracles, people are going to follow Him and we'll have a revolt, and if that happens the Romans will come in and crush us! We better get rid of Jesus now, before it's too late."

It was the raising of Lazarus that triggered the opposition against Jesus to want to put Him to death. Talk about differences, this account of the raising is not even in the Synoptics! That is a problem we must all approach.

The Differences Between John and the Synoptics on the Day Christ Died

Here is another difference: On what day of the week did Jesus die? Tradition commemorates a Friday. Today it is called Good Friday. Out of that tragic crucifixion came the good news of salvation for all mankind.

Consider another question. When Jesus was crucified, was the Passover meal future or past? The Synoptics make it clear that at that Last Supper Jesus ate the Passover meal with His disciples.

> And the first day of the unleavened bread, when they killed the Passover, his disciples said unto him, "Where wilt thou that we go and prepare that thou mayest eat the Passover?" And he sendith forth two of his disciples, and saith unto them, "Go ye into the city, and there shall meet you a man bearing a pitcher of water, follow him. And wheresover he shall go in, say ye to the goodman of the house, 'The Master saith, where is the guest-chamber, where I shall eat the Passover with my disciples?' And he will show you a large upper room furnished and prepared. There make ready for us." And his disciples went forth, and came into the city, and found it as he had said unto them. And they made ready the Passover. (Mark 14:12-16)

Jesus had the Passover meal with His disciples, then He went to the garden, was arrested, tried in a Kangaroo Court, and taken out to be crucified. When Christ was crucified, was the Passover meal past or still to come? It was past. The reader who compares that with the account in the Gospel of John is in for a shock. They do not agree.

Take a look, for example, at the Gospel of John chapter 18:28. Prior to this the Passover meal was finished, the betrayal has taken place, the hasty trial by the Jews was finished. Finally, Jesus has been turned over by the Jews to the Romans—and that is where we begin in the story.

> Then led they Jesus from Caiaphas unto the hall of judgment: and it was early; and they themselves went not into the judgment hall, lest they should be defiled; but that they might eat the Passover.

Now for John's Gospel: Was the Passover in the past or in the future? It was not past, but it was still to come. They didn't want to be defiled so they could eat the Passover. To verify this, let the reader look at John 19:14. In the middle of the deliberations of Pilate, John stops to call attention to what time it was.

What day was it? It was the preparation of the Passover... (John 19:14). And again in John 19:31 it was the day of preparation. Jesus, according to the Gospel of John, died at precisely the exact same moment as the Passover lamb was being put to death. What a difference! In Matthew, Mark and Luke at the time of Jesus' death, the Passover meal was finished. It was over. The Passover meal in John's Gospel was still to come. Translate this into days of the week and one could probably say that the Synoptics show Jesus to have died on a Friday. But John seems to suggest it was a Thursday, the preceding day. These two accounts just don't agree on the day of the crucifixion. What I am doing here is calling to the reader's attention that here is another fundamental difference.

What makes all this so complicated at times is that John seems to be trying to call his reader's attention to the fact that he is deliberately saying something other than what the Synoptics are saying.

> Now after that John was put in prison, Jesus came into Galilee, preaching the Gospel of the Kingdom of God, and saying, "The time is fulfilled, and the Kingdom of God is at hand, repent ye, and believe the Gospel." (Mark 1:14-15)

When did Jesus begin His ministry? Mark 1:14 gives the very first words of Jesus. These first words of Jesus were spoken after what took place? After John the Baptist was arrested. Keeping this in mind, turn to John 3:24. At this point Jesus was already active. He and His disciples were out baptizing. Look at John 3:24, "For John was not yet cast into prison." John seems to want to call attention to the fact he is saying something different from the Synoptics. These are things Bible students should not allow to slide by.

The Differences Between John and the Synoptics Regarding Miracles

If the reader is a serious student of Mark, one of the things that stands out in Mark's Gospel is the large number of miracles. Some scholars have concluded that as high as 60 percent to 70 percent of Mark has to do with miracles.

With this in mind, the reader should turn his attention to the fact that there are differences between the authors of John and

Mark. This is seen in two ways. First, there is a quantitative difference. What I mean by that is that John reduces the number of miracles in his Gospel. There are only seven miracles in John. There is not, in contrast to Mark, a miracle every time one turns around. So there is a quantitative difference between John and Mark.

I would like to say further, and insist that the major difference is not quantitative, but qualitative. John and Mark are seeking to say different things. To say it more simply, the miracles in Mark seem to accomplish something. They are important in their own right. They are not symbolic signs that point beyond themselves, but they actually achieve something. When Jesus fed the multitudes that in Mark is an end in itself because the people of that day were entirely convinced that the devil caused hunger on the face of the earth. When Jesus fed the multitude in Mark, what was He actually doing? He was breaking one of the bonds that Satan uses. They also believed that it was Satan who caused sickness in their day.

> And ought not this woman, being a daughter of Abraham, whom Satan hath bound, lo, these eighteen years, be loosed from this bond on the Sabbath day? (Luke. 13:16)

When Jesus healed this old lady, He was actually breaking one of the bonds of Satan. All the miracles in the Gospel of Mark are seen as ends in themselves. These miracles show Jesus in conflict with Satan, achieving victory over him.

In John however, the miracles are not ends in themselves. As a matter of fact, in the Gospel of John, they are called signs. A sign has a special purpose. It always points beyond itself. What John calls the "sign" performed by Jesus seems to have an ambiguous role in relation to believing in the revelation offered by the Christ of the Gospel.1976), [3]

As one looks carefully at the Gospel of John, there are symbolic signs that seem to point beyond themselves. For example, in Mark, when Jesus feeds the multitude, what really counts? The actual bread is what is important because it is overcoming hunger. But in John, it is not the actual bread that counts. Rather Jesus is recorded giving the discourse on, "I am the bread of life!" There is a spiritual quality that lies behind that miracle. In Mark, when Jesus healed the blind man at Jericho, He actually opened up a pair of physically blind eyes. Sickness was overcome and sickness was beaten back. But when Jesus healed blindness in the Gospel of John he said, "I am the light of the world." The miracle is no longer a miracle. It is a sign pointing beyond itself. The importance is the spiritual meaning and not the event itself.

The Differences Between John and the Synoptics Regarding Suffering

There is a different view of suffering in John's Gospel and the Synoptics. In the Old Testament, there is a principle at work that can be called the principle of retribution.

---

[3] Robert Kysar, John, the Maverick Gospel, (Atlanta: Knox, 1976), p. 67

Dr. James Kallas, in his book, The Real Satan, gives information on the meaning of the law of retribution. At this point I will use a rather lengthy quotation from Dr. Kallas:

The principle of retribution not only prevailed but dominated the Old Testament. The principle of retribution is but a fancy theological way of saying, "an eye for an eye and a tooth for a tooth."

Our problem with that principle is two fold. One, we usually see it only in negative terms. That is, we think of it only in terms of revenge. If one hurts me, puts out my eye, I have the right (even the obligation to satisfy justice) of putting out his eye. But the principle was not merely negative, allowing revenge. It was also positive, demanding reward. If someone hurt me, I could give retribution. But if someone aided me, I was to help others. Not only evil for evil but good for good.

The second problem we usually have with that principle is that ordinarily we see only its horizontal dimension, how it governs man-to-man relationships. If my neighbor hurts me, or helps me, I am to hurt, or to help him. But in Jewish thought it was not merely horizontal, governing man-to-man relationships. It was also vertical, governing the God-man relationship. If I were good in the eyes of God, he would reward me. If I sinned in the eyes of God, he would punish me. When I did right in God's eyes, he would send one of his angels of love to minister to me, look after me, and guard over me. But if I disobeyed his will, one of the avenging members of the heavenly council would swoop in on me and bring judgment on my head.

This is what we mean when we say that the Old Testament contains a religion of law, a religion of merit. Man gets what he has coming to him. His piety will affect his destiny. The good will be prospered by God and the evil will be punished. Psalm 1 is an example of this point of view. Read that Psalm and notice how its six verses are divided symmetrically into two distinct halves. The first three verses deal with the good man, the one who walks not in the ways of the wicked, and those first three verses end with the insistence that the good man "in all that he does he shall prosper." The principle of retribution, vertically understood, says that God will reward the good man. But the next three verses deal with the opposite side of the coin, concentrating on the evil man. The Psalm closes with the insistence at the end of verse six that "the way of the wicked shall perish."

The Old Testament emphasizes the conviction that God is master of the whole world that he rules through his heavenly council, rewarding the good and punishing the evil. One could measure a man's piety by looking at his wealth. If one suffered, it was because he was sinful. But the Old Testament also wrestles with exceptions to that principle. The Book of Job is a profound struggle with the inexplicable mystery of why in Job's case the principle was not true. Job was a good man, yet he suffered. Why? The problem is wrestled with, but never answered. The final "solution" of the Book of Job is to counsel us to patience, that in the mysteries of God there is a solution, but it is not known to us.[4]

---

4 James Kallas, The Real Satan, (Minnesota: Augsburg Publishing House, 1975), pp. 38-39.

Using these thoughts, according to the Old Testament suffering comes from God. He is in control. If one is good, God will bless him. If one is evil, God will cause him suffering. The idea of suffering in the Old Testament is that one is going to get what one has coming. "An eye for an eye and a tooth for a tooth." (Exodus. 21:24)

That is why the Pharisees in the Synoptics were furious with Jesus. He was spending too much time with the sinner, the sick, etc. According to the law of retribution, if a man is suffering, it is because he is evil and God is responsible for the suffering. That is the whole point of the parable of the Good Samaritan. (Luke 10) Here is a man lying out in that ditch. Who is the first man that walks by and refuses to help? The priest. He crosses over to the other side. Why? Because he is not true to his religion? No. It is because his theology is soaked with the law of retribution. He feels that if that man has met with such misfortune it is because God has allowed it and why should he help the man against God's will?

The Synoptics deliberately reverse the principle of retribution. Old Testament suffering comes from God as a punishment upon a sinner. If one reads carefully in the Synoptic Gospels, with the viewpoint of Jesus, he will see a completely different concept of suffering. With Jesus' understanding, suffering comes from Satan and is primarily directed against the saints of God. The Synoptics are saying that this world, to some undefined degree, unrolls under Satan's power. Therefore, if one sides with the forces of God, he is exposed to the attacks of the enemy. A failure to understand this difference in concepts of suffering causes all kinds of problems. For example, when most ministers preach on the beatitudes, what text do they always teach from? Everyone I have ever heard teaches from Matthew. But how do these beatitudes unroll in Luke?

> And he lifted up his eyes on his disciples, and said, Blessed be ye poor: for yours is the kingdom of God. Blessed are ye that hunger now: for ye shall be filled. Blessed are ye that weep now: for you shall laugh. Blessed are ye, when men shall hate you, and when they shall separate you from their company, and shall reproach you, and cast out your name as evil, for the Son of man's sake. Rejoice ye in that day, and leap for joy: for, behold, your reward is great in heaven: for in the like manner did their fathers unto the prophets. But woe unto you that are rich! For ye have received your consolation. Woe unto you that are full! For ye shall hunger. Woe unto those who laugh now, for ye shall mourn and weep. Woe unto you, when all men shall speak well of you! For so did their fathers to the false prophets. (Luke 6:20-26)

This is a totally different picture from what is found in Psalm 1. Instead of the righteous being like a tree planted by the waters, Jesus said, "blessed are you that are poor." Why?
Because, "your poverty has come as a direct result of serving the kingdom of God. You are poor because of the attacks of the enemy. But you are blessed because you shall be the winner in the end."

Remember Luke 13:16? Jesus talked to a crippled lady. Who did Jesus say crippled that lady? Satan.

Jesus is reversing the principle of retribution. From this point of view, look again at Luke 6:24: "But woe unto you that are rich!" Why? "Because," Jesus would say, "You are living in a world controlled by the devil, you will never get rich unless you sell your soul to the devil." Now this is not an exhaustive discussion of the principle of retribution, but it is a point of view that comes right from Jesus out of the Synoptics.

In the Old Testament, suffering is a sign of God's judgment. In the Synoptics, however, suffering is a sign of the attack of the devil. God is on the side of the oppressed. Guess where John stands? John goes back to the principle of retribution; suffering is in direct proportion to your sins. That is a completely different view from the Synoptics.

For example, in John 5:14 Jesus had just healed this crippled man. Jesus later found him in the Temple and said unto him, "Behold, thou art made whole, sin no more, least a worse thing come upon thee." He was saying that if you sin again you are going to get it in the neck again. This view is straight from the Old Testament laws of retribution. So these are the differences between the Synoptics and John's Gospel in regard to suffering.

The Differences Between John and the Synoptics Regarding Key Events In the Synoptics

Another example of differences is several key events in the Synoptics, which are missing in John. Jesus' disclosure to his disciples at Caesarea Philippi has already been mentioned. Other events missing are:

1. The Virgin Birth—missing in John
2. The Baptism—Temptation event. In John's Gospel Jesus is not baptized; the temptation is also omitted.
3. The Words of Jesus in the Garden—"Take this cup from me…"etc. Not in John.
4. The Transfiguration Scene—not in the Gospel of John.

The Differences Between John and the Synoptics regarding the Purpose of the Cross

The Synoptic Gospels portray the death of Jesus, not as an end in itself, but as a means to the victory of the resurrection.

In the Synoptics and in Paul's writings, the cross is not an end in itself. When the death of Jesus is spoken of, there is always the mention of the three days and the resurrection. Paul takes this a step further and says to the Corinthians that the beating, vibrant center of the Gospels, is not the death of Christ, but the Resurrection.

> And if Christ be not risen, then is our preaching vain, and your faith is also vain. Yea, and we are found false witnesses of God; because we have testified of God that he raised up Christ: whom he raised not up, if so be that the dead rise not. For if the dead rise not, then is not Christ raised: And if Christ be not raised, your faith is vain; ye are yet in your sins. (I Corinthians 15:14-17)

Why does Paul say this? Because of what the Synoptics teach about suffering. In the Synoptics and Paul's writings, from whom does suffering come? Suffering is an attack of Satan. Satan causes sickness, he causes hunger and he also causes death. So in the Synoptics, the death of Christ is seen as an attack by the forces of Satan. But it doesn't stop there. If one stops with just the cross, who wins the fight? Satan wins. That is why Paul says that if Jesus be not raised from the dead, Christians are most miserable and still in their sins. If there is no resurrection, what power reigns supreme? Satan's power! Paul goes on to show that Christ has been raised from the dead. Jesus has won the battle with death, hell and the grave. Satan's power has been broken. So the Synoptics never see the cross as an end in itself.

This is why the church does not worship on that special day—Good Friday. The church instead picked the resurrection day, the first day of the week upon which to worship. Every Sunday is an Easter in miniature.

Now, anyone who compares the Synoptic understanding of suffering to what is found in the Gospel of John is in for a surprise. In John, the resurrection is no longer important. What moves to the center? The cross! As a matter of fact, it is in John and John alone that Jesus says from the cross that three word sentence: "It is finished." (John 19:30) His work was completed on the cross even before the resurrection. The Synoptics never could have said that. For Matthew, Mark and Luke, Jesus' work was completed on resurrection morning.

The Differences Between John and the Synoptics Regarding the Message and Words of Jesus

If one had to summarize the message of Jesus as it is in the Synoptics in one line, what would that one line be? What did Jesus stress? The Kingdom of God! It was the focus of His first words in Mark 1:14, "Jesus came into Galilee, preaching the Gospel of the Kingdom of God." Note also the first phrase of the Sermon on the Mount: "Theirs is the Kingdom of Heaven." (Matthew 5:3) Matthew, chapter thirteen has seven parables. Every parable is about the Kingdom of God. What did Jesus teach His disciples to pray in the very first line of the Lord's Prayer? "Thy Kingdom come." (Matthew 6:10) The last words of Jesus the night before He dies are: "Verily I say unto you, I will drink no more of the fruit of the vine, until that day that I drink it new in the Kingdom of God." (Mark 14:25)

In the Synoptics, Jesus is talking about the Kingdom of God from the beginning to the end. The phrase "the Kingdom of God" is practically unknown in the Gospel of John, yet it dominates the preaching of Jesus in the Synoptics. But in John it is only mentioned but a few times.

> Not only, however, has the teaching of Jesus to the crowds and to the disciples taken on a new, unfamiliar form. Its very content seems to be altogether different. Where is the all-controlling, ever-recurring theme of the Kingdom of God? And where is the word Gospel? The later occurs nowhere; the former has almost disappeared. The phrase, "The kingdom of God" appears only at the beginning of the discourse with Nicodemus though it is echoed in the conversation with Pilate: "My Kingdom is not of this world." [5]

---

[5] Edwyn Clement Hoskyns, The Fourth Gospel, (London: Faber and Faber, 1947) p. 61.

This is not the only area of difference in regard to the Lord's message and words. Notice that when Jesus talked about the Kingdom of God, He talked about the Kingdom of God! In other words, to oversimplify it, where was Jesus pointing? To Himself, or to the Father? Jesus was pointing to the Father.

Therefore, in the Synoptics, if one takes the phrase "the Kingdom of God" literally, Jesus was always pointing beyond Himself to God the Father. There is, in other words, an area of subordination in the preaching of Jesus in the Synoptics. He was not calling attention to Himself. He was calling attention to the Father: "Our Father, who art in Heaven" (Luke 11:2).

Now compare that to what is found in the Gospel of John. First of all, the reference to the Kingdom of God is almost gone. But this note of subordination has also practically disappeared.

Jesus, in John's Gospel, did something He seldom did in the Synoptics. He pointed not to God, but to Himself. So John recorded the great "ego emie" phrases; the great "I AM" phrases. The Gospel of John continues to ring from one end to another with some of these "I AM" phrases.

"I AM's of Christ"

The Messiah (John 4:26)
The Bread of Life (John 6:35)
From Above (John 8:23)
The Eternal One (John 8:58)
The Light of the World (John 9:5)

The Door (John 10:7)
The Resurrection and Life (John 11:25)
The Lord and Master (John 13:13)
The Way, Truth, and Life (John 14:6)
The True Vine (John 15:1)

All of these appear in John's Gospel, yet they are strangely missing in the Synoptics.

These two different types of differences are found between John and the Synoptics. John seems to say very little about the Kingdom of God and shows Jesus putting Himself forward all the way through the Gospel, while the Synoptics are in direct contrast.

The Differences Between John and the Synoptics Regarding What Message Jesus Preached

Perhaps the best place to start is to ask the question: What is Jesus' favorite preaching device in the Synoptics? The answer is that He preached in parables.

I could describe a parable as a concrete picture with concrete details. It was always short, crisp and to the point, with one central truth. Jesus, in the Synoptics, spoke in concrete pictures, which are very, very short. Compare that with what is found in the Gospel of John and a different style of speaking comes to light.

For one thing, there is not a single parable in the Gospel of John. Some of the language spills over a little bit. For example, in the Synoptics, Jesus talked about the parable of the Good Shepherd who seeks out the lost sheep. In the Gospel of John similar language is there. Jesus said, "I am the good shepherd" (John 10:14), but this is not actually a parable. So there is a difference at that point.

A second difference is that this crisp, abbreviated, concrete way of speaking has disappeared. In John there are long discourses that sometimes last for chapters. For example, the speech at the Last Supper extends some three or four chapters.

Also, there is a definite pattern to all the conversations Jesus has in the Gospel of John. It goes something like this:

Action
Question
Dialogue
Monologue
Appendix [6]

That pattern is there. It is found in Jesus' talks with Nicodemus, the lady at the well, Pilate, etc.

What I am saying is that in the Synoptics, statements of Jesus are crisp, short, and concrete. In John there is kind of a leisurely, expanded, philosophical type discourse. This philosophical type discourse follows a pattern all the way through.

---

6 Eric L. Titus, The Message of the Fourth Gospel, (New York: Abingdon, 1957), p. 180.

The Differences Between John and the Synoptics Regarding the Roll of the Disciples

What I am driving at here is this: In the Synoptics, people seem to have real significance. In Matthew, Mark and Luke, there are real flesh and blood people who have a profound importance.

For example, the first character that seems to just explode on the scene out of the pages of Mark is John the Baptist. He seems to dominate the first chapter of Mark. People went flocking out to see him. He was a very important person.

In John's Gospel, John the Baptist seems to be denied any importance in his own right. He was just a voice, only a sign, and that by his own confession: "He must increase, but I must decrease." (John 3:30)

Another example: In the Synoptic Gospels, Peter is a real person. Peter played some pretty significant rolls in the Gospel of Matthew, Mark and Luke. Peter was so significant in the life of Jesus that one time Jesus was complimenting him and then turned around and denounced him. This is found in Matthew 16:17-18 and 23:

> And Jesus answered and said unto him, "Blessed art thou, Simon Bar-jona, for flesh and blood hath not revealed it unto thee, but my Father which is in heaven. And I say also unto thee, That thou art Peter, and upon this rock I will build my church; and the gates of hell shall not prevail against it! But he turned, and said unto Peter, "Get

> thee behind me, Satan, thou art an offense unto me, for thou savorest not the things that be of God, but those that be of men."

One can read the story of Peter in the Gospel of John, and he doesn't have the same kind of striking significance.

In the Synoptic Gospels the Apostles are very important, but not so in the Gospel of John.

> The most striking thing about his discussion of the community of believers is that there are no distinctions made among the believers, which might become a basis for official leadership. There is no distinction made between the role of the Apostles (the original twelve disciples) and other believers. The fourth evangelist, as a matter of fact, does not use the expression "Apostle" at all. He uses the word "disciple" where we might expect him to say "the twelve." [7]

The people in John's Gospel are not really as important. I dislike using some phrases for fear of being misunderstood. But try to see what I am trying to say.

Another example: In the Synoptic Gospels, Judas was a pretty important person. He was the one who actually turned in Jesus. He played a rather dramatic roll. In looking at John at this point, Judas seems to have faded in importance. He only made a move when Jesus told him what to do: "And after the sop Satan entered into him. Then said Jesus unto him, That thou doest, do quickly" (John 13:27). That statement shows that Jesus was in

---

7 Kysar, p. 102

total charge of the situation. "On the one hand, Judas is predestined to 'betray' Jesus as an act of divine Providence; and, on the other hand, Judas is unfit for the fellowship." [8]

This same thing showed up with Pilate. In Matthew, Mark, and Luke, Pilate had a great deal of authority. In reading the Synoptics, one gets the feeling that Pilate was in full charge of what is taking place. Whatever Pilate said was going to be important.

But what did Jesus say to Pilate in the Gospel of John? He just straight out told him that Pilate had no true jurisdiction in the whole matter. Jesus answered, "Thou couldest have no power at all against me, except it were given thee from above, therefore he that delivered me unto thee hath the greater sin." (John 19:11) Look closely, and it appears that Pilate was on trial, not Jesus.

To draw this to a conclusion, let me say, that in Matthew, Mark and Luke, there is an emphasis that Jesus was involved in an interplay of personalities. Other people were seriously affecting Him and He was having an impact on their lives. However, in the Gospel of John, Jesus is lifted above the smoke of battle. He moves in a kind of serene way, which indicated that the peace of the Father that he had before was still cast like a halo over his shoulder. He seems to be above the struggle.

There was Judas, being commissioned to do something. There was Pilate, being told he has no power. These show the serenity of Jesus, who was master of every situation. There was

---

8 Titus, p. 187

no explosion with Peter, "Get thee behind me." There was no praise for Peter. As Eric Titus puts it, "The individuals introduced in the Gospel of John in no sense emerge as strong, independent persons, but as devices to facilitate the well-defined teachings which the gospel presents." [9] Jesus seemed to be above it all. These are some of the differences between the Synoptics and John.

9 Titus, p. 34.

CHAPTER 3

Harmonizing the Differences

As I set the scene for this chapter, may the reader be reminded again that many of the differences in chapter two have been overstated. It is now the purpose of this book to begin to see how attempts have been made to harmonize some of these differences.

There are two ways to close these gaps. One is to find Synoptic ideas in John. The other is to find Johannine ideas in the Synoptics. Both have been tried. [1]

For example, when Jesus was preaching the kingdom of God in the Synoptics, He seemed to be subordinate to God. He seemed to be pointing to the Father and dismissing Himself. He was always pointing to the kingdom of God and not to himself.

However, when one looks at this closely, there is not such a sharp difference because anyone can find Johannine ideas in the Synoptics. For example:

> All things are delivered unto me of my Father: and no man knoweth the Son, but the Father; neither knoweth any man the Father, save the Son, and he to whomsoever the Son will reveal him. Come unto me, all ye that labor and are heavy laden, and I will give you rest. Take my yoke upon you, and learn of me; for I am meek and lowly in heart: and ye shall find rest unto your souls. For my yoke is easy, and my burden is light. (Matthew 11:27-30)

---

[1] Donald Guthrie, New Testament Introduction, (London: Tyndale, 1965), p. 262.

So, if one looks for Johannine ideas in the Synoptics, he finds one right here in Matthew eleven. Suddenly it appears that the differences between John and the Synoptics are not quite that sharp.

Another example: I have labored to show the difference between the location of Jesus' ministry as revealed in John and the Synoptics. John seems to show Jesus as a man of the south and the Synoptics reveal Him as a man of the north.

Yet it must be recognized that the two can be harmonized. One of the places this can be done is found in Luke 13:34. This is the kind of verse that you can skip by at first glance. But it comes to be a very important verse.

> O Jerusalem, Jerusalem, which killest the prophets, and stonest them that are sent unto thee; how often would I have gathered thy children together, as a hen doth gather her brood under her wings, and ye would not! (Luke 13:34)

Notice what Jesus said here—"how often would I have gathered thy children together…and ye would not!" What do those words of Jesus imply? That He had been down in the south before.

We will refer to Ray Summers commentary to show the reader what is meant here:

> The Synoptics contain no reference to frequent visits of Jesus to Jerusalem as they are suggested in the words "how often." John,

however, does refer to multiple visits and to the conflicts and angers Jesus faced there. There were attempts to stone him in Jerusalem on three different occasions. As a loyal Jew, He loved Jerusalem; He grieved to feel her rejection and to see her end! [2]

There again, to close the gap between the Synoptics and John one can at least see the door open in the Synoptics which allows for Jesus to have had a southern ministry.

Another example: In the Synoptics there is the story in which the disciples asked Jesus where they were to eat the Passover meal. Then Jesus told them how to find out. Note Matthew's version of the story:

> And he said, "Go into the city to such a man, and say unto him, The Master saith, My time is at hand; I will keep the Passover at thy house with my disciples." (Matthew 26:18)

Again, this suggests that the man in question knew and had clear knowledge of the Master. There was some kind of understanding between the Lord and the man. [3]

There can be found room in the Synoptic Gospels to show that Jesus did have a southern ministry.

So that leads to another assumption. If one can find material in the Synoptics to show a southern ministry, one can also find in John, material to show that Jesus had a northern ministry. As a matter of fact, John wrote in John 4:43: "Now after two days he

---

[2] Ray Summers, Commentary on Luke, (Texas: Word Books, 1974), p. 174.

[3] John Peter Lange, Langes Commentary – Matthew, (Michigan: Zondervan, 1861, p. 469.

departed thence, and went into Galilee." There is a visit to the north. Another verse that makes this clear is found in John 7:1: "After these things Jesus walked in Galilee: For he would not walk in Jewry, because the Jews sought to kill him."

Attempts to harmonize can be made. One of the differences discussed in Chapter 2 was that in the Synoptics the speech of Jesus was usually brief, crisp, and short. And in John it usually expanded and was lengthy. However, that is not a hard and fast rule. What is the long discourse in the Synoptics? The Sermon on the Mount. It lasts for three chapters. So, the gap can be closed there too!

As the reader looks at all these extreme differences that have been indicated, one becomes aware that some of these can be pulled together. After having pulled some of these differences together it may be recognized that there are many ways that these differences can be harmonized. Yet the reader will find himself faced with the fact that while the gap can be narrowed, it can never be bridged in full. There always remains a modicum of material, which cannot be harmonized or brought together without really straining the text.

One of the differences, which just cannot be harmonized, is the day Christ died. Did Jesus die before or after the Passover meal? C.K. Barrett makes clear how impossible it is to reconcile the conflict at this point.

> John differs from the Synoptic Gospels also in the date, which he gives for the crucifixion. According to Mark (followed by Matthew

> and Luke) the Last Supper was a Passover meal; that is, it was eaten in the early hours of Nisan 15; the arrest and trial took place in the same night and in the course of the next (solar) day Jesus was crucified. All these events took place on Nisan 15 (which extended, in the year of the passion, from about 6 p.m. on a Thursday to 6 p.m. on Friday). According to John 13:1; 18:28; 19:14,31,42 (see the notes also) the crucifixion happened on Nisan 14, the day before the Passover; the Last Supper must have been eaten the preceding evening. Thus the events are set a day earlier than in Mark, and the Last Supper is no longer the Paschal meal; Jesus died at the time when the Passover sacrifices were being killed in the Temple. Here again is a real contradiction; it seems impossible to reconcile the dates. [4]

Another fact that cannot be harmonized, is the turning point that caused the Jewish authorities to move against Jesus. The writer stated that in the Synoptic Gospels it was the cleansing of the Temple that caused the Jews to move against Jesus. In John, the cleansing of the Temple is moved from the close of the ministry of Christ to the early part of His ministry. John makes it clear that the raising of Lazarus lay behind the motive of the plot to kill Jesus. Again, C.K. Barrett says that these differences just cannot be resolved.

> An important historical difference between John and Mark (followed by Matthew and Luke) lies in the motive, which is suggested by the two evangelists for the final and successful plot of the Jewish authorities against the life of Jesus. In Mark 11:18 it is stated that when the chief priests and scribes heard of the cleansing of the Temple they sought how they might destroy Jesus. This bold challenge provoked their hostility and brought about the final crisis.

---

[4] C.K. Barrett, The Gospel According To St. John, (Philadelphia: Westminster, 1955), p. 48.

> But in John the cleansing of the Temple is described in chapter 2, and can therefore have had nothing to do with the final plot of the Jews. John, on the other hand, narrates at length the raising of Lazarus, an incident not mentioned by any of the Synoptics but treated by him as decisive in the machinations of the Jews against Jesus. There is a contradiction here, which cannot be completely resolved. It does not seem probable that there were two cleansings of the Temple, one at the beginning and the other at the end of the ministry. [5]

One can go a long way in bringing the Synoptics and John together, but there always remains a small area that cannot be harmonized. This then brings up the next point for consideration. As a consequence of the differences between John's Gospel and the Synoptic Gospels, two completely different ways of interpreting John have been around since the very dawn of the church.

One of these is associated with Clement of Alexandria. He was a church Father who lived in the city of Alexandria in Egypt about the year 150 to 215 AD. [6] Clement of Alexandria, fully aware of the broad distinction between the Fourth Gospel and the earlier Gospels said that the Gospel of John is strictly a "theological" work. [7]

What Clement was saying was that he felt that John was a spiritual Gospel. He called the author "the theologian." Therefore, when there is a difference between the Synoptics and John, Clement always relied on the Synoptics for historical facts.

---

[5] Barrett, p. 47.

[6] John W. Brush, Who's Who In Church History, (New York: Abindon, 1962), p. 17.

[7] Edwyn Clement Hoskyns, The Fourth Gospel, (London: Faber and Faber, 1947), p.17.

Many schools of thought have embraced this way of looking at the Gospel of John, even right down to the Twentieth Century in the University of Tubingen in Germany. Such schools of thought say that John isn't so much historical observation as theological confession. Now that is one point of view. To summarize this point of view in a word, I would describe it as "non-historical." So in the quest to speak to the differences that occur due to John's spiritual imagination, historically, it is not reliable.

There is another view, diametrically opposed to that view of Clement. It grew up about the same time through a man named Irenaeus. He lived in the years 140 AD to 202 AD. He was the Christian Bishop at Lyons (now in France). He was also active in the fight against the Gnostic Sects about that time. [8]

Irenaeus of Lyon constantly used the Gospel of John as a defense against Gnosticism. Not to go into detail, let me summarize what a Gnostic believes. Jesus was only spirit and not a true human, and this world is evil. The early Christian creeds were hammered out in opposition to the teaching of Gnosticism. [9]

In effect, Gnosticism denied the true humanity of Jesus. What makes all this important is that Irenaeus quoted from the Fourth Gospel time and time again to prove that Jesus was truly human. Irenaeus always pointed to the Gospel of John to prove

---

8 Brush, p. 35.

9 Donald T. Kauffman, The Dictionary of Religious Terms, (New Jersey: Revell, 1967), p. 211.

the historicity of Christ. [10] Some of the quotes in the Gospel of John, which show that Jesus was a true human being are:

1. "And the Word was made flesh." (John 1:14)
2. "Jesus saith unto her, Give me to drink." (John 4:7)
3. "Jesus wept." (John 11:35)

In these simple examples it becomes clear that Jesus was truly human. Why did He sit down by the well? He was tired. He asked for water because he was thirsty. He was human. Why did he weep? He loved those people. Jesus, being human, felt like they felt.

This is the kind of material that Irenaeus came to again and again. In other words, when Irenaeus was pushed to the wall he would insist that John is historical. John has a solid body of good historical information. This is not just an argument that goes on between the liberal and the conservative wings of the church. How does one interpret the Gospel of John, historically or spiritually?

All this leads to another question, which is related to this: Did John know the Synoptic Gospels? What view does the reader think Clement took? Did John know or did he not know the Synoptics? Clement said that yes, John did know the Synoptics and he borrowed from them. [11]

---

10 Hoskyns.

11 Christian Frederick Cruse, The Ecclesiastical History of Eusebius Pamphilus. (Michigan: Baker, 1969), p. 234.

Clement's arguments explain to the satisfaction of many scholars why there are so many differences between John and the Synoptics. First of all is his answer to the question: Why are there so many omissions? Because John knew and had the Synoptics before him. John made so many omissions because those incidents have already been covered in the other Gospels. Then why does John add things occasionally? Maybe John picked up some information over the years that he wanted to add. Why does John alter material in the Synoptics? Simply to bring out the spiritual meaning of some of these events.

Did John know the Synoptics? Clement would say yes, John knew them and leaned on them. John therefore was dependent on the Synoptics.

On the other hand, Irenaeus would take the opposite view. He would say no, John did not lean on the Synoptics for his material. He would argue that John was more historical and when there were any differences, the Gospel of John would be more reliable.

Both of these views have been in existence for many years. Now I will discuss the attempt to handle these differences and where I stand in these two streams of thought.

What I would like to do in this book is to try and find a balance between these two positions. The position I attempt to develop for the reader is as follows:

I agree with Clement that John did know the Synoptics.

I also argue that John knew more than the Synoptics. He had read the Synoptics, but was not dependent upon them alone.

Because he knew the Synoptics and because he knew the life of Jesus as an eyewitness, he was able to recognize that sometimes the other three Gospels were being misunderstood. Therefore, the direction I will take to solve the problem of differences between John and the Synoptics that cannot be harmonized is this: As John wrote, he wrote not to contradict, not to overpower, not to reject the Synoptics, but he wrote in order to correct possible misinterpretation and misunderstandings which had grown up out of the Synoptic Gospels themselves.

I am going to show how the Synoptic Gospels have been misunderstood and misapplied, and I am going to give my own interpretation to show the reader what the Synoptic Gospels were really trying to say.

John knew the Synoptics, but he knew more than they did. He understood that the church was coming up with wrong interpretations. So his intention was to correct the wrong interpretations that had been given to the Synoptic Gospels.

The next step is to see how John went about this task under the inspiration of the Spirit.

CHAPTER 4

John Corrects Toward History and He Corrects Away From History

Now I shall draw the reader's attention to how John carefully sought to correct any misunderstanding regarding the Synoptics—at least in the areas where the Synoptics were being misunderstood.

As John corrected the Synoptic Gospels, he did so in two ways. The first of these ways the reader will have no difficulty understanding. John corrected toward history. What I mean by that is that in some places John's Gospel is definitely found to be more historical, more accurate and more reliable than the Synoptics. Because John had been with Jesus, he knew more than the other writers did. So, one way that John corrected was toward history. This book gives a few examples later.

The second way that John corrected for things that had been misleading in the Synoptics is a bit more difficult to get a hold of, but what I mean will be made clear. John corrected away from history. What is meant by that is, perhaps at times John's Gospel is less reliable and less historical than the Synoptics, but it is more theological.

At this point, this book will assume that the Fourth Gospel is a thorough going interpretation of Jesus. At no point is this assumption, weakened by the tendency to mix history and interpretation. [1]

I present that John did know and had read the Synoptic Gospels. They had been circulated for a generation. However, John did not lean upon them. He was independent of them because the evangelist who wrote the Gospel was none other than the Apostle John. Therefore, he did not have to lean on what, for him, would be secondary sources. Rather, as he wrote, he was writing precisely because he did know the Synoptics and he knew as the Synoptics stood they were in some places causing problems, which demanded comment and further explanation.

John's basic purpose for writing was not to discredit, nor reject the Synoptic Gospels, but to re-claim a threatened literary heritage because they were starting to pose questions, which no one had ever addressed.

> More consciously than the Synoptics John writes from the vantage point of the resurrection and with the aid of hindsight as well as the Spirit (see John 2:21-22; 7:39; 11:51-52; 12:16; and the Paraclete sayings in chapters 14-16). This is why he does not refrain from adding his own commentary to Jesus' words, and projects onto the Lord's deeds light which comes from the life of the church. He often gives to the miracles (earlier wonder-stories which he has taken over as part of the tradition) an undeniable sacramental significance.
>
> Note also the use of the perfect tense in the logic of Jesus, e.g., 6:63—"the words that I have spoken to you are spirit and life." This refers to the word of Christ as administered by the Church. Mention

[1] Eric Lane Titus, The Message of the Fourth Gospel, (New York: Abingdon, 1957), p. 7.

> of the Spirit indicates that the Church is already a realized fact, and the perfect tense shows that Jesus' own earthly mission of preaching the word is now something accomplished. [2]

Now these questions would take another book to cover fully, but we will look at a few just so the reader may become familiar with the proper methods for handling the differences between the Synoptics and the Gospel of John.

In the simplest form of the story, the writer John was sitting in Ephesus about the year 90 AD. [3] The Synoptics had been circulating for several years and they had been read and re-read. Yet they were being misunderstood. Problems were arising and so John wrote to correct some of those problems.

John was not writing to reject the Synoptics, but to reject some of the spurious interpretations that had been given to the Synoptics. He made these corrections in two different ways. First he made corrections toward history. The second thing he did was to correct away from history. I brought this out earlier, but the reader must be clear as to where we are going with all these differences.

It is time to give a few examples concerning how John corrected toward history. When one reads the Gospel of John, he is carried into a more intimate and understandable and

---

2 Ralph P. Martin, New Testament Foundations: A Guide for Christian Students, (Michigan: Eerdmans, 1975), p. 273.

3 Charles Caldwell Ryrie, Biblical Theology of the New Testament, (Chicago: Moody, 1959), p. 309.

comprehensible understanding of history than the Synoptics actually give.

Begin by looking at John 19:13. This verse at first glance is not going to shatter anyone, because it is not a profound verse theologically. Yet it does come to have some enormous significance in the history of the Fourth Gospel. All I want the reader to see in this verse is one little geographical fact that often slips by.

> When Pilate therefore heard that saying, he brought Jesus forth, and sat down in the judgment seat in a place that is called the Pavement, but in the Hebrew, Gabbatha. (John 19:13)

John wrote that Jesus was judged in a place called the Pavement. That one verse for centuries was one of the great pillars of the liberal critical theology, which argued that the Gospel of John could not have been written by the Apostle John. These scholars argued that Matthew does not mention the Pavement, and neither does Mark. And no paved place had ever been discovered, so it was just assumed that the author of the Fourth Gospel had reported on something of which he was totally ignorant, because there was no paved place in Jerusalem.

Guess what happened in 1933? They found the Pavement. It now serves as a floor in the basement in the Convent of the Sisters of Sion. [4] It is clear that John knew more than the Synoptics. He moved closer to history. When this Pavement became an archaeological find, suddenly it brought the Gospel of John into

---

[4] J.W. Packer, gen. ed. New Testament Illustrations, (Cambridge: University Press, 1966), p. 57.

sharp focus as being more historical and more reliable than had previously been believed. It comes closer to history than the others do.

Another example: Take a look at John 5:2:

> Now there is at Jerusalem by the sheep market a pool, which is called in the Hebrew tongue Bethesda, having five porches.

For centuries, this verse too was one used to show that the Gospel of John talks in terms of imagination. Clement would say that this is the theologian speaking. Some of these writers said that the five porches represented the five books of Moses, etc. One author said that the roofed walkways were put there for the sick to lie on. Nature has provided remedies, but men must provide hospitals. [5]

Why did these authors dismiss this as theological interpretation? Because they had never found the five colonnades. Archaeologists found the five porches in 1888. [6] Again, John comes far closer to history than do the Synoptics. This Gospel was written by a man who was there. And now modern archaeological discoveries are proving this point.

Here is one more example of how John moved closer to history. What makes this so impressive is revealed in the following question: Are these items at the heart of the Gospel or

---

5 Matthew Henry, Matthew Henry's Commentary on the Whole Bible, (Virginia: MacDonald, 1921), p. 919.

6 Packer, p. 58.

are they just casual remarks? They are casual remarks. The writer of John is at home with his material. He knew Jerusalem so well he could just toss these remarks off like they were nothing. Look at John 3:23:

> And John also was baptizing in Aenon near to Salim, because there was much water there: and they came, and were baptized.

Now from the Synoptics, it is clear that John was baptizing in the Jordan. On the other hand, the Fourth Evangelist mentions in a casual manner, the place where he baptized and why.
This is something most readers would just skip over. By the way, I was told a few years ago, that underground springs have been discovered in Aenon. This would show why there was plenty of water there.

John did this again and again. He moved toward history. Many things would never have come to light if it were not for the historical facts that John's Gospel contains. Many of his statements make the Synoptics more understandable.

Up to now, I have given a few examples of how John corrected toward history. In John's Gospel there are more historical facts than are found in the Synoptics. It is my purpose now to tackle that, which is more difficult to understand, that is, how John corrected away from history.

May I alert the reader to the fact that this is just one man's attempt to solve some of these differences between the Synoptics and John. If the reader disagrees, the reader and I may still rejoice in their common salvation by faith rather than theology.

I am convinced of this: A document must be taken on its own terms. The Bible must be taken on the terms of the people who wrote it. At this point, John was not just pushing historical facts. He wanted his readers to see that Jesus is the Son of God, and if the facts got in the way and did not make clear what he truly meant, John then interpreted the facts for his readers. He even wrote that he was not all that bothered by historical facts.

> And many other signs truly did Jesus in the presence of his disciples, which are not written in this book; but these are written, that ye might believe that Jesus is the Christ, the Son of God; and that believing ye might have life through his name. (John 20:30,31)

What John said is this, "Jesus did a lot of things I didn't even bother to write down. But, what I did write was intended to bring you into the faith." Dr. G. E. Ladd makes this clear by the questions he asked.

> The solution that lies closest to hand is that the teachings of Jesus are expressed in Johannine idiom. This is an easier conclusion than to think that John's style was assimilated to Jesus' style, and that John wrote his epistle in the idiom he learned from Jesus. If this is the correct solution, and if we must conclude that the Fourth Gospel is couched in Johannine idiom, this important question follows: To what extent is the theology of the Fourth Gospel that of John rather than that of Jesus? To what extent has the teaching of Jesus been so assimilated in John's mind that what we have is a Johannine interpretation rather than an accurate representation of Jesus' own teaching? [7]

Some of the differences between John and the Synoptics are due to the theological emphasis, which John gives to certain events. It is difficult to avoid the conclusion that John reflects a larger measure of theological interpretation than do the Synoptics.

The final chapter of this book will give a few examples of how John changed historical facts in order to make a theological point. Why did John feel he could correct away from history?

Again, Dr. G. E. Ladd gives a very interesting insight into what might be the answer to this question.

> Another solution is that John deliberately recast and interpreted the words of Jesus to fit his own contemporary situation, sensing behind his work the authority of Jesus himself, now glorified and risen from the dead, continuing to instruct his people through the Spirit (John. 14:26; 16:12). Another solution is that Jesus was too great a teacher to be limited to a single style and idiom of teaching. Possibly he used a vivid, picturesque, parabolic style with the crowds in Galilee and a more profound, extended form of discourse with the more educated people of Jerusalem and with his own disciples. It is possible that in the last days Jesus in fact used a different style that opened up the deeper truths of his person and mission to his disciples, and John deliberately cast the entire Gospel in this idiom. [8]

I have attempted to solve this most difficult problem regarding some of the differences by showing that:

---

[7] George Eldon Ladd, A Theology of the New Testament, (Michigan: Eerdmans, 1974), p. 215.

[8] Ladd p. 220

1. John sometimes corrected toward history, because he knew more than the Synoptics.
2. John also corrected away from history to get across a theological point. He played footloose and free with the facts to make his point.

CHAPTER 5

Why John Corrects Away From History And Conclusions

In an effort to summarize, the reader must look at a few examples of how John corrected away from history.

What I am arguing is that John knew the Synoptics, but he also knew more than the Synoptics. So one of the reasons he wrote was to try and preserve the Synoptics and clarify their meaning.

Therefore, many of the places where the Gospel of John differs from the Synoptics can be attributed to the fact that John knew more about the personal life of Jesus than did the Synoptic writers.

I claim that John sometimes corrected the Synoptics by bringing them closer to history. He was able to supply details and motives and geographical details that the Synoptics had not given.

Also, it is my conviction that another way to see these differences is in the fact that John not only corrected toward history, but that he also corrected away from history.

To explain this, I will go back to the conviction that the key to these differences is found in the fact that all people, no matter what their skin color, think in Greek terms and in Greek thought.

The scriptures were not written by Greeks. They were written by Jews. The Jews had a different way of looking at things. A Greek would be more interested in looking at historical, objective facts. The Hebrew was interested in the subjective meaning of those facts. Therefore, the Hebrew writer found himself, when he could bring out that subjective meaning, playing footloose with the raw objective facts. He was not all that bothered by precise historical accuracy. He was more concerned with the meaning of the facts.

That is what I mean when I say that John corrected away from history. Many times, John changed some of the details in the Synoptics and the way a story was told, not because he was indifferent to the Synoptics, but because he wanted to bring out the real subjective inner meaning of what the Synoptics were trying to say.

A few examples of what I am talking about may be helpful here. These examples are not exhaustive, only illustrative. These examples, let me remind the reader again, are just to show how to deal with some of the differences that are discussed in chapter 2. This book will not be able to go into the heart of the Gospel or go chapter by chapter, but I do wish to give the reader a look at where John hung his reader's thoughts and why.

For example, John omitted some very important key events in the life of Jesus. One of those key events is His virgin birth. John also omits the Baptism/Temptation as recorded first in the Gospel of Mark. Why? I believe that John omitted them because he was trying to bring out the true sense of what the Synoptics were trying to say, but by the time he wrote, that true sense had been obscured.

What is being said will be clear as you look to the scriptures themselves. Look at Mark chapter one, the account of the Baptism story as Mark saw it, noticing verse eleven. After Jesus came up out of the water, what did the voice from heaven say? It did not say, "He is my beloved Son." "A voice from heaven said, 'You are my beloved son; you are my delight.'" (L.N.T.P.)

The voice was speaking to Jesus. The voice said, "You Jesus—You are my Son." Now that is the way Mark expressed himself. I claim that the reason Mark expressed himself that way is that he was writing his Gospel to the powerful Roman people. And he wanted to stress to the Romans, who respected power, that Jesus is God's own representative. So Mark showed the voice of God speaking to Jesus Himself: "You and I Jesus, we are in this together, we shall overthrow the devil and all his works and all his ways." One can see why Mark phrased himself that way. Now, can the reader see what possible misinterpretation can come out of Mark? The voice is directed to Jesus. How could one misinterpret that sentence? It could be taken to imply that Jesus up until that moment didn't know that He was the Son of God! And from early Christian records it is apparent that that misinterpretation soon appeared. This is what led to the early theory of adoptionism.

> Adoptionism was one of the christological errors. According to this view Christ was originally a man who, by a special decree of God,

after having been thoroughly tested, was given supernatural powers by the Holy Spirit at the time of His baptism. [1]

It came to be claimed very early on that up until the moment of Jesus' baptism He was only a human. At the baptism His divinity began.

That was one kind of problem that Mark put in front of the early church. Matthew and Luke seem to have been very sensitive to that problem. They then had to know that Mark was being misread and being misinterpreted.

So Matthew and Luke had at least one motive in adding the virgin birth stories. They were trying to slam the door shut on the theory of adoptionism. After adding the virgin birth narratives, it was no longer possible to say that Jesus became divine at the baptism, because He was already divine as of His birth. So this was their attempt to refute adoptionism. But were they completely successful? No! They were not, because while it was no longer possible to say that Jesus became divine at the baptism, it was possible to argue that Jesus apparently became divine at His birth. So there still remained a dateable moment in time as to when Jesus' divinity actually began.

Now, John had that problem in front of him. I am convinced that John omitted the baptism and virgin birth stories because they had been misleading. He therefore corrected away from history. He didn't even discuss the historical events, but tried to bring out

---

[1] A. E. J. Rawlinson, The New Testament Doctrine of the Christ, (Michigan: Baker B

the meaning of those earlier writers. What were Matthew, Mark and Luke trying to get across? That Jesus was truly divine.

So John omitted the events themselves and insisted upon the meaning behind the events. What is the first line of the Gospel of John from this point of view? "In the beginning"—and that is supposed to remind the reader of Genesis 1:1, before the world ever came into being. To make sure the reader doesn't miss the point, in chapter one, verse two, John actually mentioned the creation story. "In the beginning was the Word, and the Word was with God, and the Word was God." (John 1:1) Skipping down to verse fourteen, the reader finds: "And the Word was made flesh, and dwelt among us, (and we beheld his glory, the glory as of the only begotten of the Father) full of grace and truth."

One can actually see what John was trying to do. He was moving away from history. He was correcting away from history. His purpose was to bring out the meaning of the earlier documents, which had been misunderstood. This is what John did over and over in his Gospel. That is why he left some events out, added others and changed what other writers were saying. Thank God for John's Gospel.

Further examples to show how John corrected away from history come in the form of two events, which occur toward the close of Jesus' ministry that John left out of his Gospel entirely:

1. Jesus in the garden. Matthew 26:36-46
2. The Transfiguration. Matthew 17:1-13

When Jesus was in the garden of Gethsemane, He said these words, "O My Father, if it be possible, let this cup pass from me." (Matthew 26:39) What did this emphasize about Jesus? It showed His humanity and His humility.

During the Transfiguration scene, the voice from heaven said: "This is my beloved Son, in whom I am well pleased, hear ye him." (Matthew 17:5) What did that event emphasize? It emphasized Jesus' divinity.

So here are two events. One speaks of Jesus' humanity and the other emphasizes His glory. May I remind the reader, that even if these two events were very important in the Synoptics, John still left them out of his Gospel and moved away from history.

With these two events that speak of the humanity and the glory of Jesus, the Synoptics have something that the Jewish mind can understand because a Jew always thinks in concrete terms. But, a Greek thinks in abstract terms. [2]

In a classroom today, if you were asked to write the number infinity, you could use that little eight flipped over on its side, or, you could say a number raised to the nth degree. Now, this is Greek abstract language. The Hebrew does not think in abstract terms. He thinks in concrete terms. For example: How did Jesus get across the idea of infinity? In Matthew 18:21-22 Peter came up to the Lord and asked Jesus,

---

2 James Kallas, A Layman's Introduction to Christian Thought, (Philadelphia: Westminster, 1974), p. 37.

> "Lord how oft shall my brother sin against me, and I forgive Him? Till seven times?" But Jesus said to him, "I say not unto thee, until seven times: but, until seventy times seven."

What did Jesus mean? Is He to be taken literally? Was Peter supposed to take a little piece of papyrus and keep a record till he reached 490 times? After that was he to forgive no more? Obviously not. What was Jesus doing? He was speaking in typically concrete Jewish fashion. Jews didn't have a little eight to flip over on its side; they didn't have nth degree. They used concrete pictures. The Jew understands infinity by multiplying 10x10x10.

Now, if the reader remembers that the Hebrew thinks concretely, then for the Jew the glory of Jesus is described by one event, the Transfiguration scene. The Hebrew can look at that one concrete event, the Transfiguration, the glory of Jesus, and he will know that Jesus is always the Son of God, glorified, the transcendent Son of the Father. He can look at the one event of His humiliation, "Father take this cup from me," and looking at the one event, he will know that Jesus was always living a life of humiliation and true humanity.

The Hebrew has no problem understanding that those events are illustrations of larger truths, but the Gospel of John was not written to Jews. It was written in Ephesus and the audience was Greek in thought. They thought abstractly. So John had a whole new set of problems he had to deal with.

Again, let the reader be reminded that the problem we are working on is to see how John moved away from history to give and show the true meaning of the Synoptics. Therefore, if John took the Transfiguration scene and discussed that by itself, the Greek audience could think that that was the only moment that Jesus was the glorious Son of God. So what John did was to move away from history, omit the events of the Transfiguration, and try to get across the idea that Jesus is always the Son of God. John did this in passages like John 1:14:

> And the Word was made flesh, and dwelt among us, (and we beheld his glory, the glory as of the only begotten of the Father,) full of grace and truth.

This word glory (doxa) implies a continuous glory: they were always beholding His glory. Raymond E. Brown, in his book "The Gospel According to John," describes it this way:

> The concept of the glory of God in Old Testament thought offers important background for Johannine use. In the Old Testament there are two important elements in the understanding of the glory of God: It is a visible manifestation of His majesty in acts of power. While God is invisible, from time to time He manifests Himself to men by a striking action, and this is His kabod or glory. Sometimes the action is in the realm of nature, e.g., a thunderstorm. Sometimes it takes place in history. In Exodus 16:7-10, Moses promises the people: "In the morning you shall see the glory of God."" He is referring to the miracle of the manna to be performed by God. God's glory is in the cloud whereby His presence becomes visible to the Israelites in their desert wanderings (Exodus 16:10), and also in the fire. (Exodus 24:17)

Since Jesus is the incarnate Word of God, he is an embodiment of divine glory. The two elements of kabod are present in him. He represents the visible divine presence exercising itself in mighty acts. More than the Synoptics, John insists that this doxa was visible during the ministry and not only after the resurrection. It is true that John does not describe the transfiguration, which for the Synoptics is really the only manifestation of glory during the public ministry. (Luke 9:32) Yet John does stress that the divine doxa shone through Jesus' miraculous signs. [3] (John 2:11; 11:40; 17:4)

This idea is also dealt with by C. K. Barrett in his book, "The Gospel According to St. John": The clearest example of Christ's Glory was the Transfiguration (Mark 9:2-8), an incident which is not recounted in John. John 1:14 nevertheless asserts that the glory of God was manifested in Jesus. [4]

The glory of Jesus was not confined to one event. Wherever men saw Jesus, they were continually beholding the glory of God. John omitted the event. He corrected away from history, but his purpose was to bring out the true glory of Jesus.

For the same purpose he omitted the event of suffering in the garden, because Jesus didn't suffer only then. It was not only then that His true humanity was revealed. John removed that event.

He brought in a whole new series of events to get across the humanity of Jesus. There are events in the Gospel of John that are not found in the Synoptics that display a continuing reference to the humility and humanity of Jesus.

3

4 C. K. Barrett, The Gospel According to St. John, (Philadelphia: Westminster, 1955), p. 166.

3 Raymond E. Brown, The Gospel According to John, (Doubleda, 1966), p.503.

When Jesus met the lady at the well he told her, "I'm thirsty." (John 4:7) When his friend Lazarus died, He wept (John. 11:33, 35). John was showing that Jesus was human. He was correcting away from history.

For another example, in the Synoptics there are many miracles. Every time one turns around there is another miracle. In the Gospel of Mark Jesus was healing everyone who came to Him.[5] There is a big difference between John and the Synoptics regarding the miracles.

First of all, there is the qualitative difference. The miracles are no longer ends in themselves they are only signs. Also there is a quantitative change. They are reduced down to the symbolic number of seven. Why? I believe it is because John was again moving away from history. There is no question that Jesus performed a lot more miracles than John would write about (John 20:30-31).

> And many other signs truly did Jesus in the presence of his disciples, which are not written in this book: But these are written that ye might believe that Jesus is the Christ, the Son of God; and that believing ye might have life through his name.

Why did John move away from history at this point? Because, the way I understand this, the miracles are open to two or three misunderstandings!

---

[5] Raymond E. Brown, The Gospel According to John, (Doubleday, 1966), p. 503.

One possible misunderstanding is this: The miracle stories heaped one on top of the other could reduce Jesus to simply a kind of a wizard or a carnival or a sideshow. John does not want his reader thinking of Jesus as a wizard or a sideshow. As a matter of fact, John brought in some strong evidence denouncing that interpretation. Look at John 6:2. "And a great multitude followed him, because they saw his miracles which he did on them that were diseased."

They did not come for spiritual edification. They did not come to gain new insights into the relationship between God and man. Rather they came because it was a dry dusty place to live, and nothing ever happened there. So they went out to watch Jesus, the carnival show, hoping he would straighten out a few legs, etc. A great multitude followed him because they saw the miracles he did upon those who were in need.

Simply following Jesus does not make one a follower of Jesus. Jesus Himself said that, "Not every one that saith unto me, Lord, Lord, shall enter into the kingdom of heaven" (Matthew 7:21). John was denouncing that point of view when he made the statement in John 6:2, and said it again at the end of the miracle. Look at John 6:14-15:

> Then those men, when they had seen the miracle that Jesus did, said, "This is of a truth that prophet that should come into the world."
> When Jesus therefore perceived that they would come and take him by force, to make him a king, he departed again into a mountain himself alone.

What John's Gospel is saying is that yes, Jesus was a Prophet—a powerful person. However, what did the crowds want to do with that power? They wanted to use it. They would make Him a king, but Jesus perceived what they were doing. He turned His back on anybody who would try to commercialize those miracles.

This is one of the reasons why John played down the miracles. If you look closely at miracles today, in some cases where men have capitalized on them I personally feel it has hurt the cause of Christ.

Another reason John played down the miracles is that in the Synoptics, the way they were related lead to a misinterpretation. An illustration will help make this point clear. A man goes into the grocery store to get a few items for his wife just before dinner. While in the store, a mother has a little child who is toddling up and down the store isles. The child comes up and pulls out a can of soup on the bottom of a large stack of cans. What happens? Cans of soup go everywhere! The whole display tumbles down. The man in the store who is picking up a few things for his wife is not subjectively involved. In fact, he thinks it a bit amusing. Cans all over the place! The mother is subjectively involved. She turns red and is very upset. She is embarrassed. She is actively involved. It does not bother the man. Why? Because he is not subjectively involved. He can look at it as a disinterested spectator.

There are many times one can look at the miracles of Jesus as a disinterested spectator. Here is a person with a devil, or a person that is crippled. Who does the miracle involve? Those people in need. One can look at the miracle as a disinterested spectator because he is like the man in the store. He is not subjectively involved. This is not the greatest illustration, but ponder it awhile. John did not want his reader at any time looking at Jesus in a disinterested way, like He is some kind of a bug on a pin that can be examined without any personal commitment. So what John did was to change the whole concept of what the miracles are all about.

For example, the number one miracle that Jesus did in the Synoptics was the casting out of demons. Yet there is not one casting out of demons in the Gospel of John. Why not? Because it is too easy to be objective. One can see somebody possessed with a demon, beating himself with a chain, and rolling himself in the fire affected by Jesus' power. But Jesus' power does not affect the observer because he doesn't have a demon.

So what did John do? He completely changed what it means to be demon possessed. John did not let anyone look at Jesus in a disinterested, objective way. For John, demon possession in the Gospel is unbelief! Jesus said, "Ye are of your Father the devil." (John 8:44) Why? Because these men did not believe in Jesus. [6]

Johannine thought says that one cannot possibly see Jesus go by and not get involved. What is the most cutting, critical form of to be confronted with Jesus and say no! That is demon possession in John.

---

[6] C. K. Barrett, The Gospel According to St. John, (Philadelphia: Westminster, 1955), p. 166.

Why are there differences that cannot be reconciled between the Synoptics and John? Because John so often moved away from history to give his reader the true meaning. Why did John feel like he could do this with his facts? Because John was saying that the greater creative genius behind his Gospel was none other than Jesus Himself.

> Another solution is that John deliberately recast and interpreted the words of Jesus to fit his own contemporary situation, sensing behind his work the authority of Jesus himself, now glorified and risen from the dead, continuing to instruct his people through the Spirit. [7] (John 14:26; 16:2)

A third reason John corrected away from history and changed the miracle stories was to bring out the true meaning. Mark told so many miracle stories that in one sense Mark became his own worst enemy. After reading Mark, the reader's head may be left swimming. One might ask the question, "Which of these miracles are most important?" Here is one raising the dear, another miracle of feeding the hungry. Over here is a miracle of healing.

Those miracles are all stacked together almost one on top of the other.

After reading Mark you see that there is no graduation; there is no indication of what is the primary miracle. You could ask the question, "What is more important, a full stomach or a victory over death?" The Gospel of Mark does not make that clear because it just lumps the miracles side by side.

---

[7] C. K. Barrett, The Gospel According to St. John, (Philadelphia: Westminster, 1955), p. 166.

John not only cut down the number of miracles but he raised them in ascending order of importance. What is the climax of the Christian proclamation? The Resurrection of Jesus over death. So what was the last sign that Jesus performed in the Gospel of John? The raising of Lazarus from the dead in John chapter eleven.

John has moved away from the historical facts to give his readers the great meanings of these events in the life of Christ.

All of the problems that I have sought to cover have been problems that arose from within the Synoptic Gospels. Matthew, Mark and Luke created their own problems. These problems all came from within the church from the early writing.

John was also facing many problems that arose outside the Synoptics and came upon the Apostle from outside the church. These problems caused John to move away from history and create other differences that this book does not have room to consider. It is my conclusion that the Fourth Evangelist intended to present his readers with a written expression that puts the Lord's life in proper perspective. This Gospel is different, attractive, and mysterious. It is my hope that in some way I have helped beginning students and searching Christians to new insights concerning the differences between John and the Synoptics.

The Author

Jack was in the Navy for four years during the Korean War. When he came home he enter Life Bible College in Los Angeles. After graduation he pastored several Four Square churches.

Jack and his wife, Darlene, took a group of people on a tour to the Holy Land where they went first to Cairo, Egypt to see the Pyramids, then to all the wonderful places where Jesus traveled and then crossed the Mediterranean Sea to Grease. A trip like that puts new insights into Bible study.

Jack goes back to school and obtains his Masters and Doctors degree at the California Graduate School of Theology in Glendale, California while he was on the preaching staff with Dr. Stuart McBirnie at the United Community Church in Glendale. It was at this time that he began the writing of this book.

Jack later started an independent church in San Marcos, California. He also pastored an American Baptist church in Morongo Valley, California and Hope Baptist Church in Phoenix, Arizona.

www.ingramcontent.com/pod-product-compliance
Ingram Content Group UK Ltd.
Pitfield, Milton Keynes, MK11 3LW, UK
UKHW040558210726
13854UKWH00008B/1392